ORIGAMI
OF THE SEA

DOVER PUBLICATIONS, INC.
MINEOLA, NEW YORK

To access the video tutorials, type the following link:
http://www.nuinui.ch/video/it/f28/origami-del-mare

Bibliographical Note

Origami of the Sea, first published by Dover Publications, Inc., in 2019,
is an unabridged English translation of the work originally published by
NuiNui, Switzerland, in 2018.

International Standard Book Number

ISBN-13: 978-0-486-83233-3
ISBN-10: 0-486-83233-3

Manufactured in China
83233301   2019
www.doverpublications.com

Text, diagrams, and videos
Vanda Battaglia
Pasquale D'Auria
Francesco Decio
Marc Kirschenbaum
Nick Robinson

• •

Photographs
Dario Canova
Nick Robinson

Contents

Instructions

Choosing paper

Square-shaped sheets of paper are usually used when creating origami models. Once you run out of the enclosed paper, you may purchase more in hobby shops or on the Internet.

- The best option would be purchasing large sheets of paper and then sizing them down to smaller square dimensions. This provides remarkable savings.
- Normally origami paper is two-toned: colored on one side and white on the other.
- You may use sheets of paper with different patterns and colors when creating the origami models in this book.
- Origami paper with a wide variety of patterns may be found on the market: choose the kind that is best suited to the origami model that you have chosen.
- We suggest trying your hand with less expensive paper before working on the final origami model with your finest paper.

How to fold

- Arrange the sheet of paper on a hard smooth surface, possibly on a well-illuminated table, and make sure you have enough space for comfortable elbow movement.
- Always remember that paper is a very sensitive kind of material and that once you make a fold, then it is practically impossible to eliminate all traces of the same.
- Prepare every fold with extreme care: take all the time you need, concentrate on your work and make sure that the paper is perfectly arranged on the work surface.
- When you are ready, take the lower edge of the paper and slowly lift it to the upper edge, always keeping the sheet of paper steady on the work surface with your other hand.
- When the two edges are perfectly aligned, start flattening the folds by delicately pressing them with a light movement in the direction of the fold.
- Finally complete the fold: in order to have a distinct and well-defined finish, press the edge with the back of your fingernail (usually using the thumb).
- Many prefer folding origami paper outward rather than inward, so that their hands do not get in the way.

Techniques

Name of the symbol	Aspects of the symbol	Application of the symbol	Result of the application
Valley fold			
Valley and unfold			
Mountain fold			
Mountain and unfold			
Repeat the crease once, twice, three times, etc.			

Name of the symbol	Aspects of the symbol	Application of the symbol	Result of the application

Name of the symbol   *Aspects of the symbol*   *Application of the symbol*   *Result of the application*

Fold to dotted line

Inside reverse

 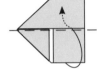 

Hidden edges (to X-rays)

  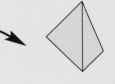

Turn over

Push, press, turn inside

Name of the symbol	Aspects of the symbol	Application of the symbol	Result of the application
Rotate the origami in a different direction			
Fold the bisector of a corner			
Crimp			
Symmetrical crimp			
Unfold one or more folds, one or more layers			

Name of the symbol	Aspects of the symbol	Application of the symbol	Result of the application

Name of the symbol	Aspects of the symbol	Application of the symbol	Result of the application
Enlarged origami			
Reduced origami			
Fold at 90°	90°		
Bulge			
Transition to three-dimensional	3D		

video: http://www.nuinui.ch/video/it/f28/origami-del-mare/p12

Blue Whale

Marc Kirschenbaum

The blue whale, whose name comes from the Greek and means "big wings," is a cetacean of the baleen whale family. The blue whale is the largest living animal in the world.

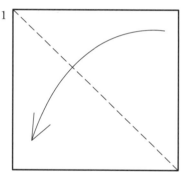

Valley fold along the diagonal.

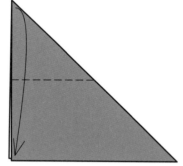

Valley fold the top corner down.

Valley fold along the angle bisector.

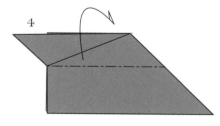

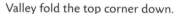

Form a mountain fold that is parallel to the bottom edge.

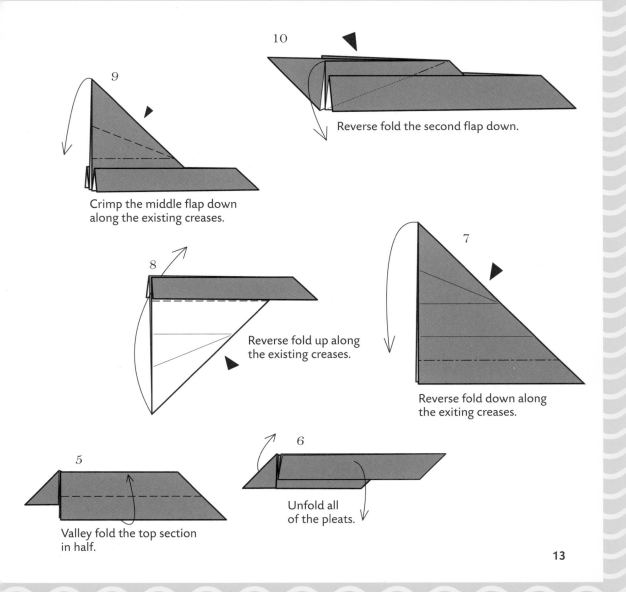

9 Crimp the middle flap down along the existing creases.

10 Reverse fold the second flap down.

8 Reverse fold up along the existing creases.

7 Reverse fold down along the exiting creases.

5 Valley fold the top section in half.

6 Unfold all of the pleats.

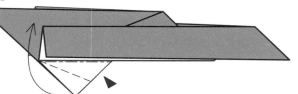

11

Reverse fold up, and then down
again along the angle bisector.

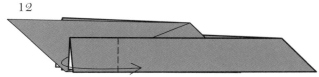

12

Valley fold the flap over as far as possible.

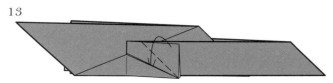

13

Tuck the flap into the back pocket.

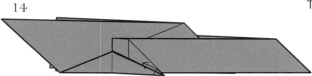

14

Valley fold the tip of the flap in.

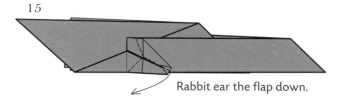

15

Rabbit ear the flap down.

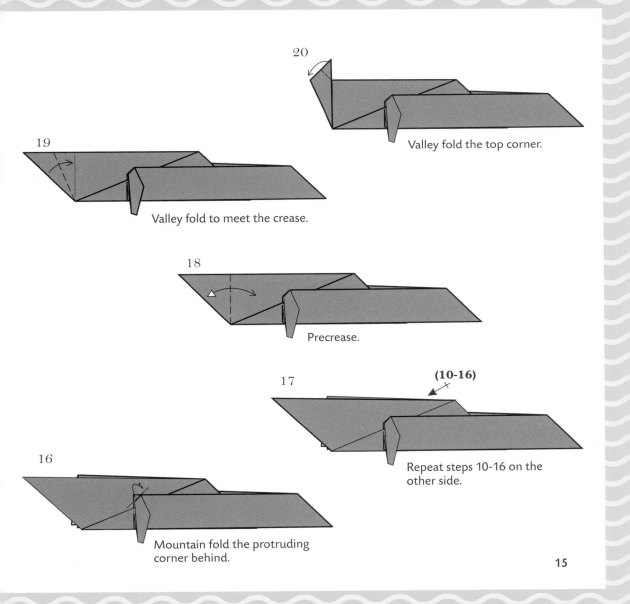

20

Valley fold the top corner.

19

Valley fold to meet the crease.

18

Precrease.

17

(10-16)

Repeat steps 10-16 on the other side.

16

Mountain fold the protruding corner behind.

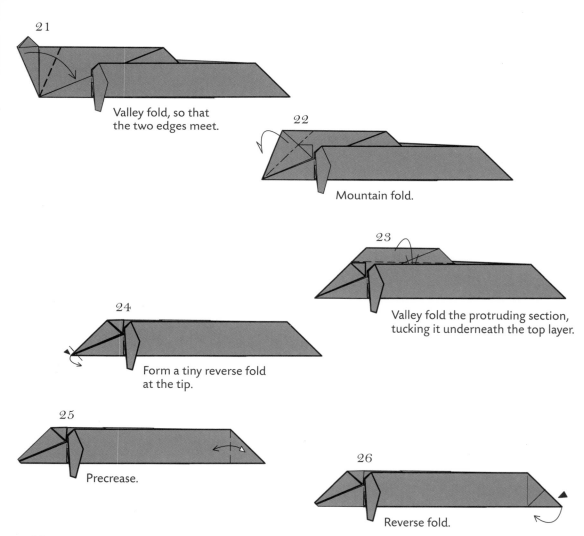

21 Valley fold, so that the two edges meet.

22 Mountain fold.

23 Valley fold the protruding section, tucking it underneath the top layer.

24 Form a tiny reverse fold at the tip.

25 Precrease.

26 Reverse fold.

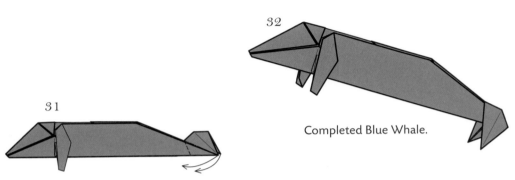

32

Completed Blue Whale.

31

Crimp the tail section down.

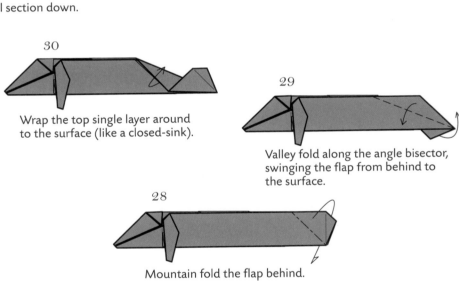

30

Wrap the top single layer around
to the surface (like a closed-sink).

29

Valley fold along the angle bisector,
swinging the flap from behind to
the surface.

28

Mountain fold the flap behind.

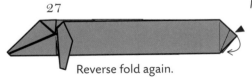

27

Reverse fold again.

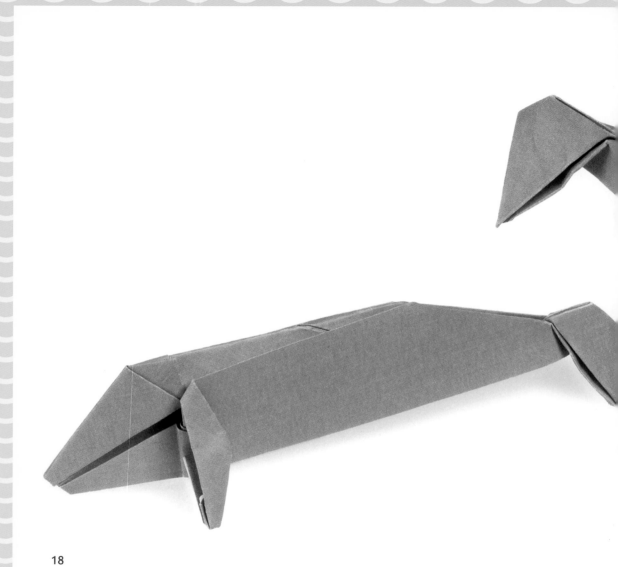

video: http://www.nuinui.ch/video/it/f28/origami-del-mare/p20

Penguin

Pasquale D'Auria

Penguins are aquatic birds and great swimmers. They used to fly in the past, but today no penguin species is capable of flight. This origami model reproduces the penguin in the typical position it assumes when on land.

Fold the paper along both diagonals, bringing the top corners over the opposite ones and unfold, then turn the origami over.

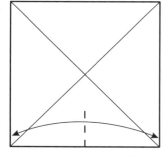

Fold bringing one side over the opposite one, mark the spot and unfold.

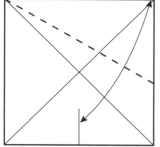

Fold bringing the corner on the fold you just made, and unfold.

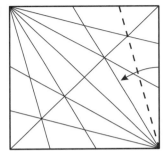

8

Fold bringing the edge to the crease.

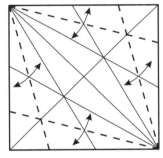

7

Fold bringing the edges to the creases and unfold.

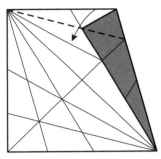

9

Fold bringing the edge to the crease.

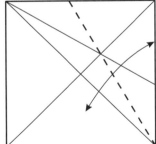

4

Begin this crease below the corner and make it pass exactly where the two previous folds meet, then unfold.

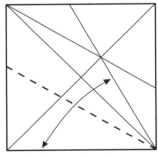

5

Fold bringing the edge to the crease and unfold.

6

Fold bringing the edge to the crease and unfold.

21

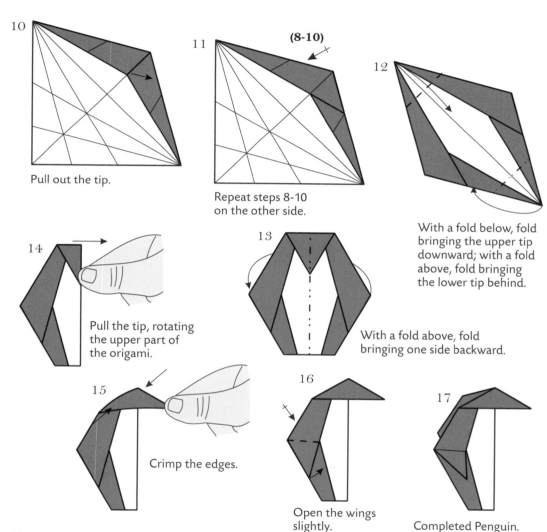

10

Pull out the tip.

11

(8-10)

Repeat steps 8-10
on the other side.

12

With a fold below, fold
bringing the upper tip
downward; with a fold
above, fold bringing
the lower tip behind.

14

Pull the tip, rotating
the upper part of
the origami.

13

With a fold above, fold
bringing one side backward.

15

Crimp the edges.

16

Open the wings
slightly.

17

Completed Penguin.

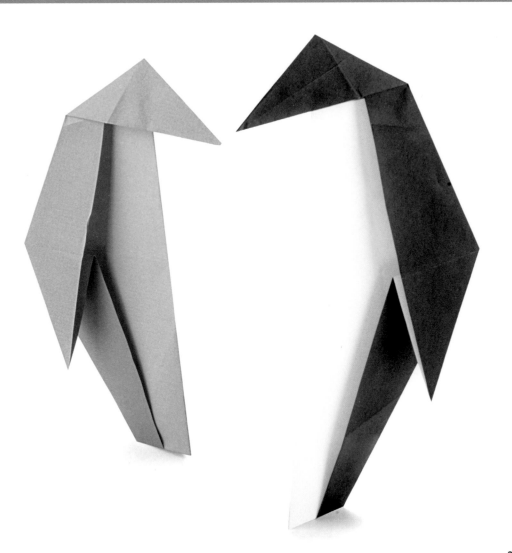

video: http://www.nuinui.ch/video/it/f28/origami-del-mare/p24

Shark

Pasquale D'Auria

We harbor lots of prejudice and fear about this predator, which this origami model reproduces in its typical attacking position.

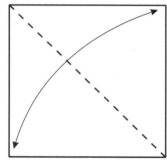

Fold the paper in half bringing the top corner over the opposite one and unfold.

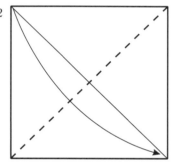

Fold the other corner over the opposite one.

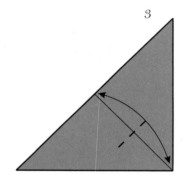

Only lift the first layer of paper upward, mark the spot and unfold.

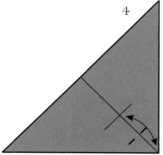

Only lift the first layer of paper upward, mark the spot and unfold.

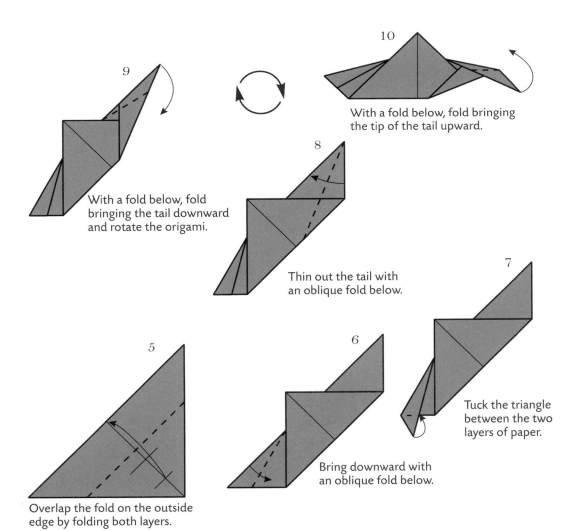

10

With a fold below, fold bringing the tip of the tail upward.

9

With a fold below, fold bringing the tail downward and rotate the origami.

8

Thin out the tail with an oblique fold below.

7

Tuck the triangle between the two layers of paper.

5

Overlap the fold on the outside edge by folding both layers.

6

Bring downward with an oblique fold below.

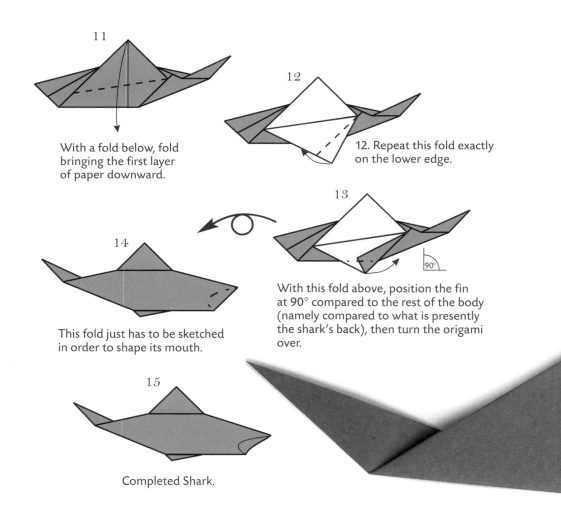

11

With a fold below, fold bringing the first layer of paper downward.

12

12. Repeat this fold exactly on the lower edge.

13

With this fold above, position the fin at 90° compared to the rest of the body (namely compared to what is presently the shark's back), then turn the origami over.

14

This fold just has to be sketched in order to shape its mouth.

15

Completed Shark.

video: http://www.nuinui.ch/video/it/f28/origami-del-mare/p28

Common Eagle Ray

Pasquale D'Auria

The common eagle ray is a cartilaginous fish that can grow to be over six feet long and weigh about thirty pounds. This origami model shows the typical pose of the ray when it moves through the sea, as if it were flying.

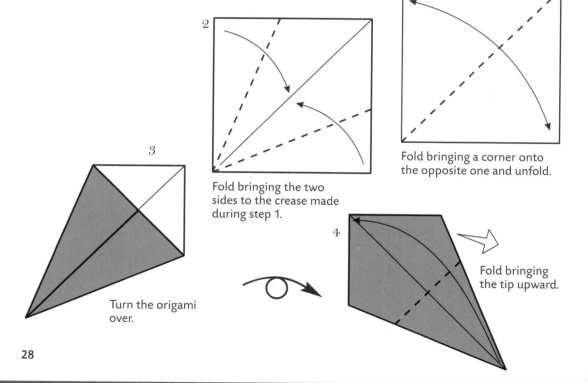

Fold bringing a corner onto the opposite one and unfold.

Fold bringing the two sides to the crease made during step 1.

Turn the origami over.

Fold bringing the tip upward.

8

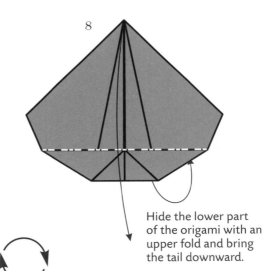

Hide the lower part of the origami with an upper fold and bring the tail downward.

7

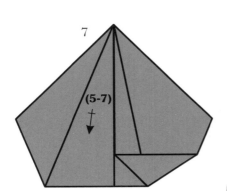

(5-7)

Rotate the origami and repeat steps 5-7 on the other side.

6

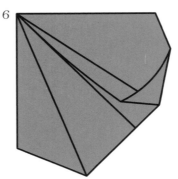

Intermediate step: now press the lower layer.

5

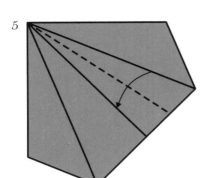

By making this fold, the lower layer will tend to roll.

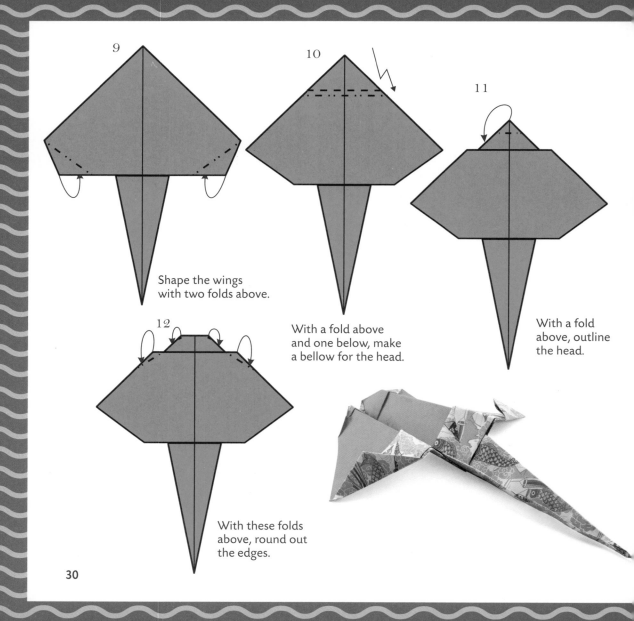

9

Shape the wings with two folds above.

10

With a fold above and one below, make a bellow for the head.

11

With a fold above, outline the head.

12

With these folds above, round out the edges.

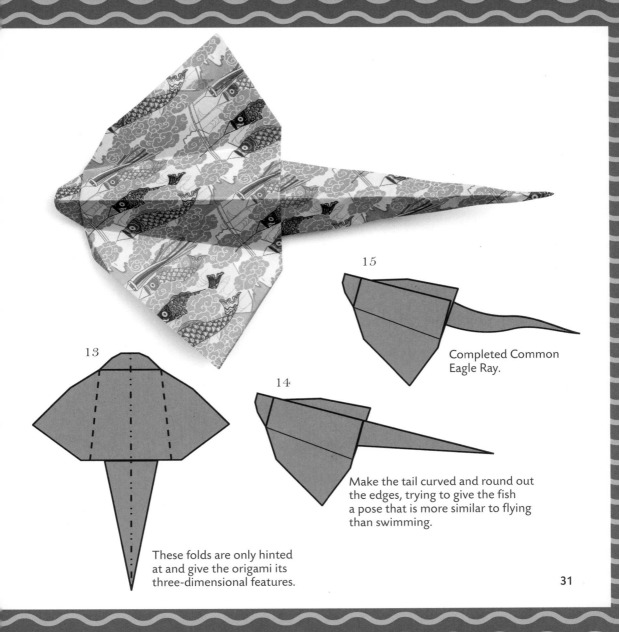

15

Completed Common Eagle Ray.

13

14

Make the tail curved and round out the edges, trying to give the fish a pose that is more similar to flying than swimming.

These folds are only hinted at and give the origami its three-dimensional features.

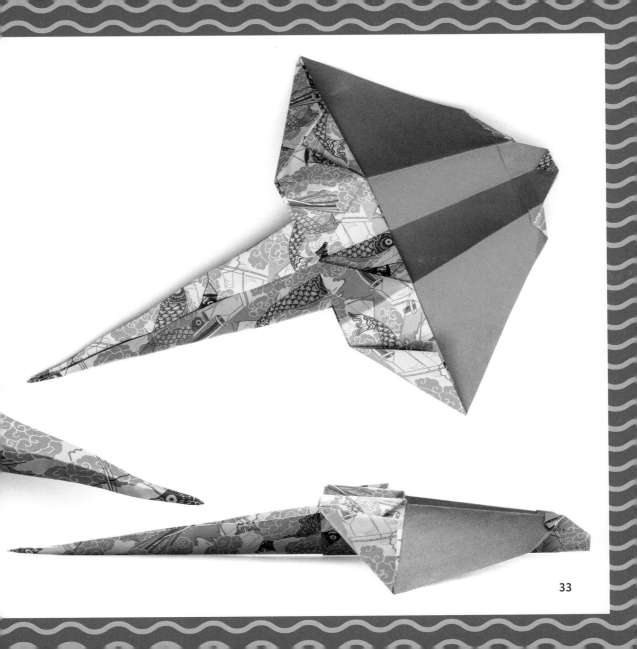

video: http://www.nuinui.ch/video/it/f28/origami-del-mare/p34

Deep-Sea Fish

Pasquale D'Auria

We know very little about deep-sea fish. This version of a classic origami model highlights its teeth, which is the best known feature of these fish. It also creates a fish that appears to be swimming.

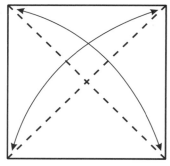

1

Fold bringing one corner onto the opposite one and unfold, then repeat on the other corner.

2

Fold bringing the external edges onto the central crease, and unfold.

3

Fold bringing the external edges onto the central crease.

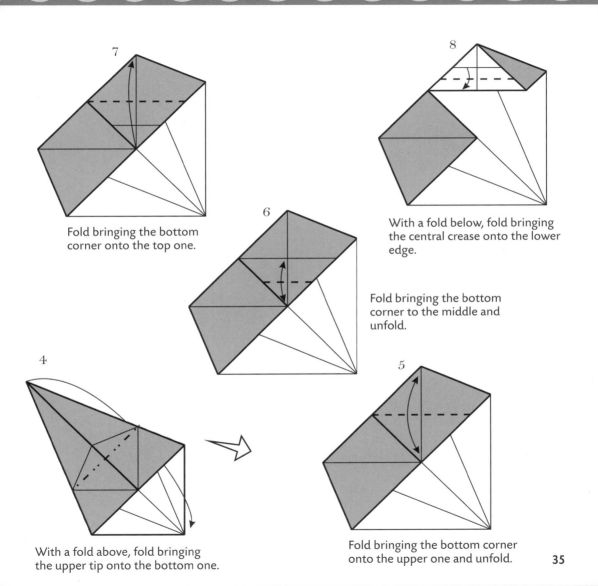

7

Fold bringing the bottom
corner onto the top one.

6

Fold bringing the bottom
corner to the middle and
unfold.

8

With a fold below, fold bringing
the central crease onto the lower
edge.

4

With a fold above, fold bringing
the upper tip onto the bottom one.

5

Fold bringing the bottom corner
onto the upper one and unfold.

35

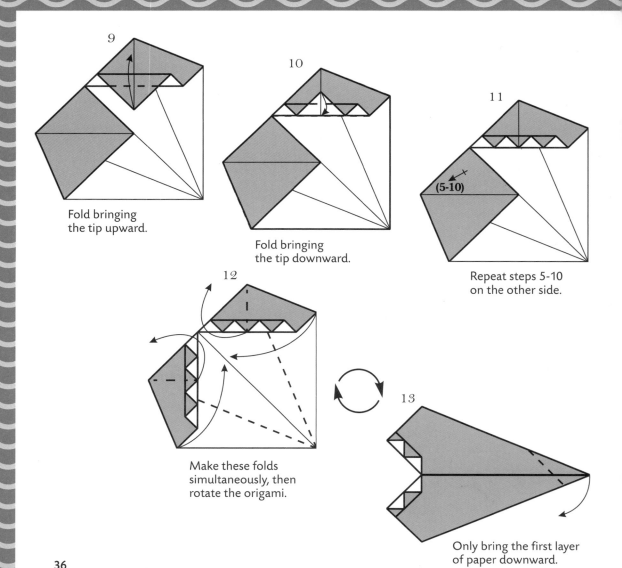

9 Fold bringing the tip upward.

10 Fold bringing the tip downward.

11 (5-10)

Repeat steps 5-10 on the other side.

12 Make these folds simultaneously, then rotate the origami.

13 Only bring the first layer of paper downward.

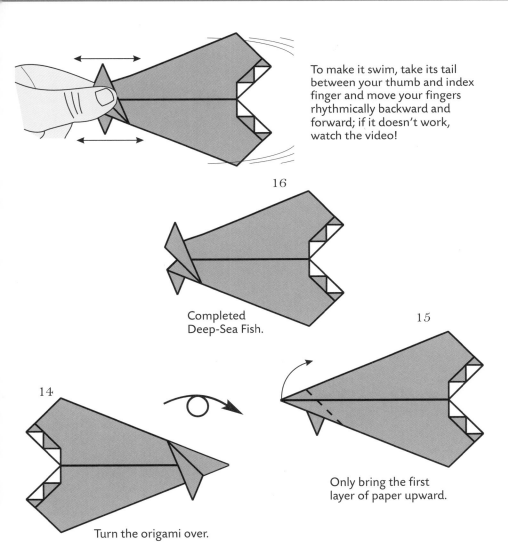

To make it swim, take its tail between your thumb and index finger and move your fingers rhythmically backward and forward; if it doesn't work, watch the video!

16

Completed Deep-Sea Fish.

15

Only bring the first layer of paper upward.

14

Turn the origami over.

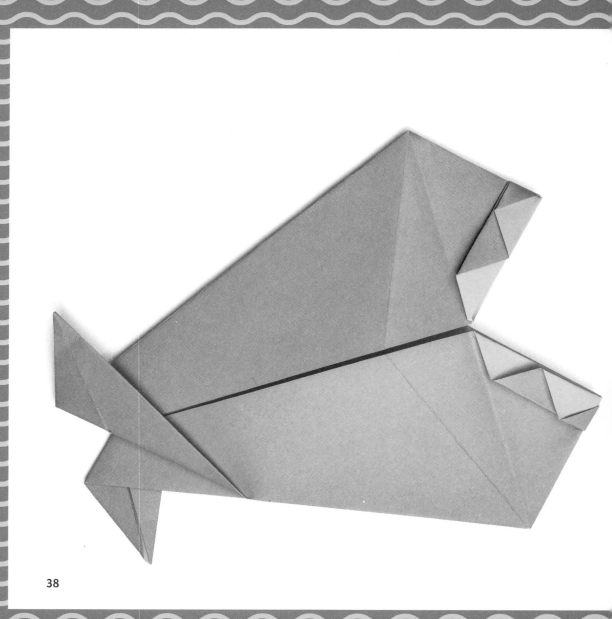

video: http://www.nuinui.ch/video/it/f28/origami-del-mare/p40

Simple Fish

Nick Robinson

This origami project is a modern version of a classic model. It is relatively simple to create, and you obtain an easily recognizable fish.

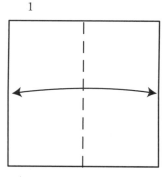

White side up, fold in half, then unfold.

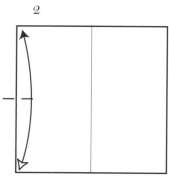

Make a small pinch to mark the center point.

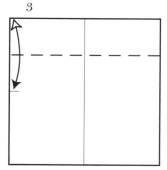

Fold the upper edge to the pinch, crease, and unfold.

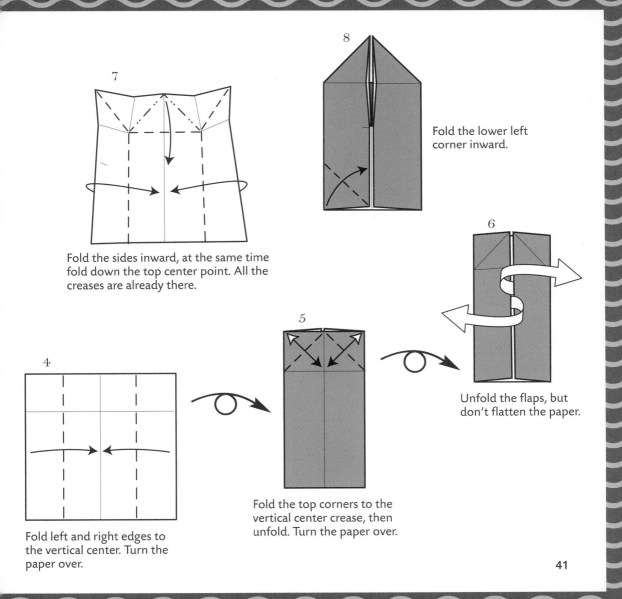

7

Fold the sides inward, at the same time fold down the top center point. All the creases are already there.

8

Fold the lower left corner inward.

6

Unfold the flaps, but don't flatten the paper.

4

Fold left and right edges to the vertical center. Turn the paper over.

5

Fold the top corners to the vertical center crease, then unfold. Turn the paper over.

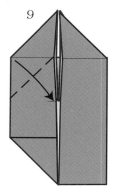

9

Fold the corner to the
pinch mark.

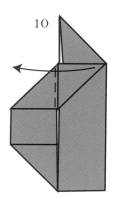

10

Fold a single flap
to the right.

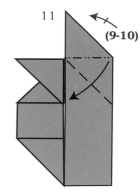

11

(9-10)

Repeat steps 9-10
on the right.

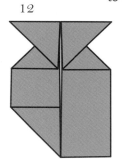

12

The model so far.
Turn the paper over.

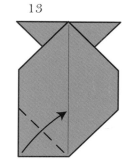

13

Fold a corner inward.
Rotate the paper.

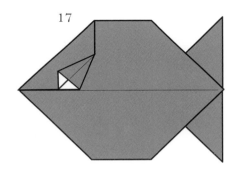

Completed Simple Fish.

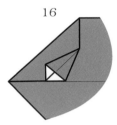

The eye is complete.

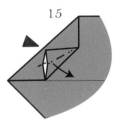

Lift the flap and squash it open.

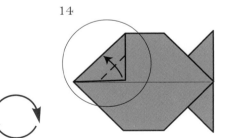

Fold over the corner.

video: http://www.nuinui.ch/video/it/f28/origami-del-mare/p46

Squid

Nick Robinson

This is an unusual model, traditional, yet little known. And when you are finished, you can put your fingers inside the mouth and round the body out to make it three-dimensional.

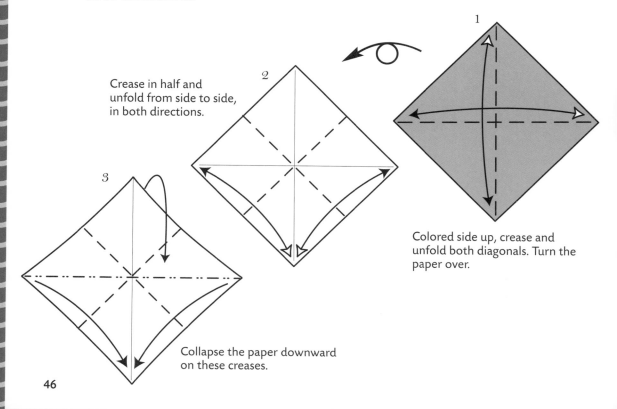

Crease in half and unfold from side to side, in both directions.

Colored side up, crease and unfold both diagonals. Turn the paper over.

Collapse the paper downward on these creases.

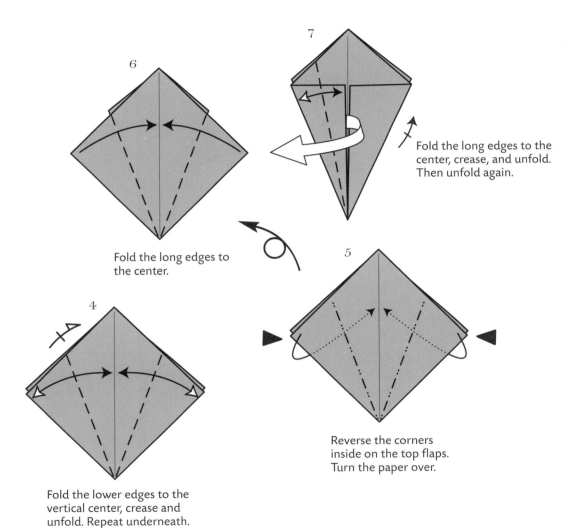

6

Fold the long edges to the center.

7

Fold the long edges to the center, crease, and unfold. Then unfold again.

4

Fold the lower edges to the vertical center, crease and unfold. Repeat underneath.

5

Reverse the corners inside on the top flaps. Turn the paper over.

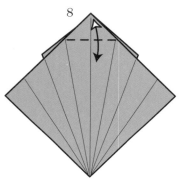

8

Crease and unfold a
triangular flap at the end
of the inner creases.

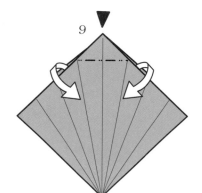

9

Open and flatten the top
corner. The paper is now
three-dimensional.

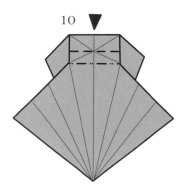

10

Make a valley in the center,
flattening the paper.

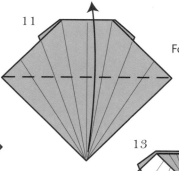

11

Fold up a single layer.

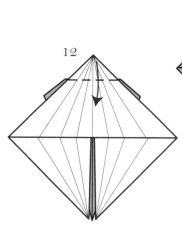

12

Fold a flap down along
a hidden edge.

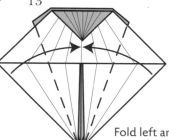

13

Fold left and right edges to
the center.

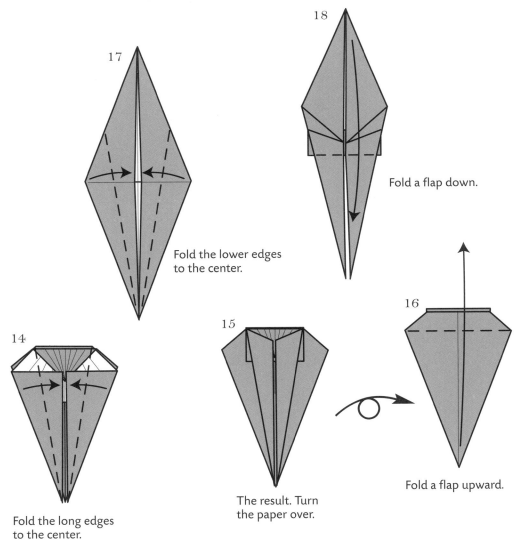

17

Fold the lower edges
to the center.

18

Fold a flap down.

14

Fold the long edges
to the center.

15

The result. Turn
the paper over.

16

Fold a flap upward.

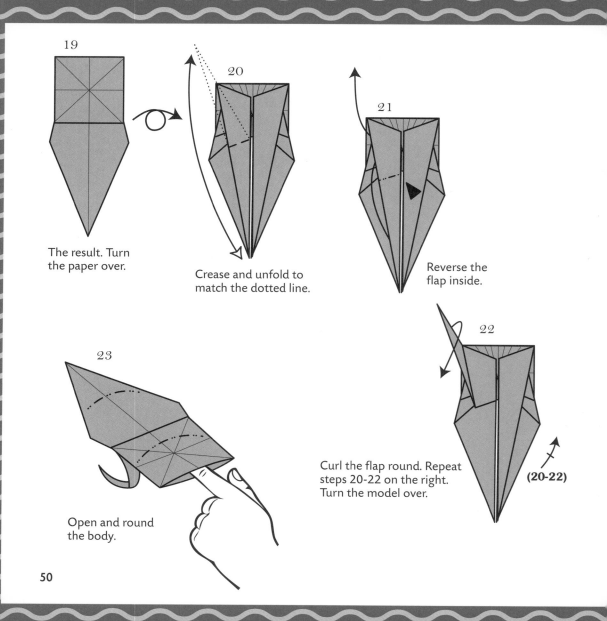

19

The result. Turn the paper over.

20

Crease and unfold to match the dotted line.

21

Reverse the flap inside.

22

Curl the flap round. Repeat steps 20-22 on the right. Turn the model over.

(20-22)

23

Open and round the body.

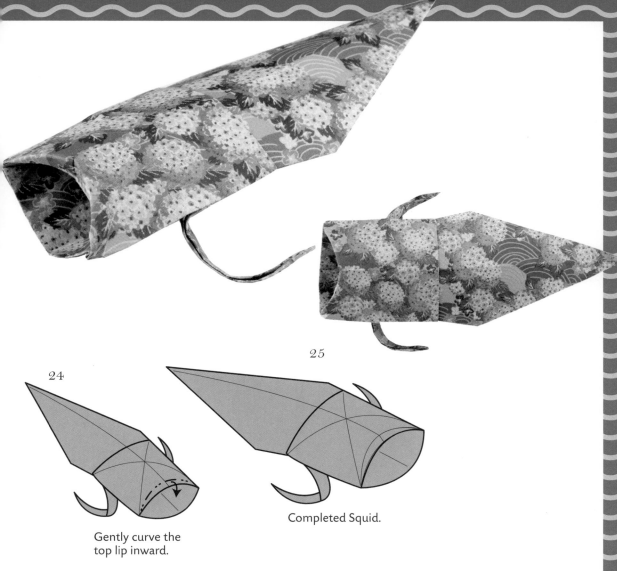

24

Gently curve the
top lip inward.

25

Completed Squid.

video: http://www.nuinui.ch/video/it/f28/origami-del-mare/p52

Small Boat

Francesco Decio and Vanda Battaglia

In some parts of Japan a unique ceremony takes place during the time dedicated to honoring the memory of the dead: many little boats are placed into ponds, streams, rivers, and even the ocean. According to legend, these little boats travel to the realm of the dead and bring the spirits of the deceased back to the land of the living—but only for a short period of time. This origami model is inspired by that ancient tradition.

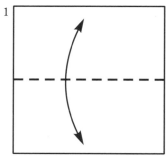

Valley fold, bringing the top corner over the opposite one and unfold.

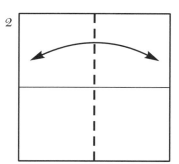

Make a vertical crease by folding the right side over the left one and then unfold.

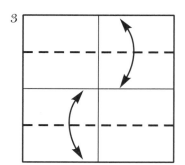

Fold bringing the lower and upper external edges onto the central crease and then unfold.

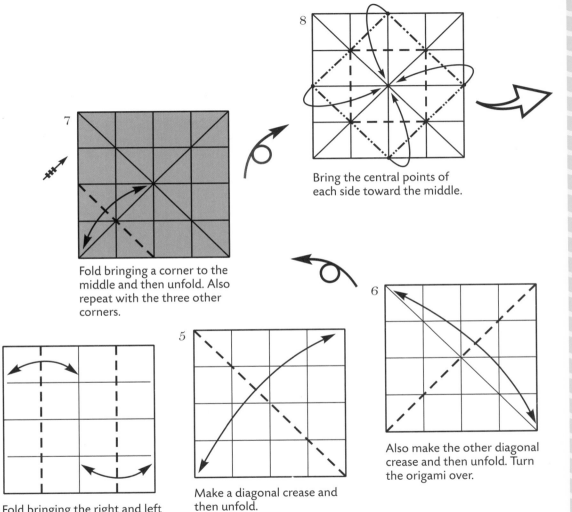

7

Fold bringing a corner to the middle and then unfold. Also repeat with the three other corners.

8

Bring the central points of each side toward the middle.

6

Also make the other diagonal crease and then unfold. Turn the origami over.

4

Fold bringing the right and left sides over the vertical crease and then unfold.

5

Make a diagonal crease and then unfold.

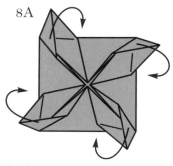

8A

The drawing is enlarged compared to the previous one. After having brought the central points toward the middle, lower the layers onto the backing surface according to the direction of the arrows, until you obtain the figure shown in step 9.

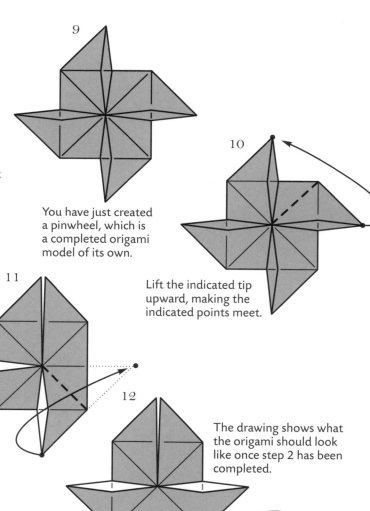

9

You have just created a pinwheel, which is a completed origami model of its own.

10

Lift the indicated tip upward, making the indicated points meet.

11

Lift the indicated tip once again, toward the right, as indicated by the dotted lines.

12

The drawing shows what the origami should look like once step 2 has been completed.

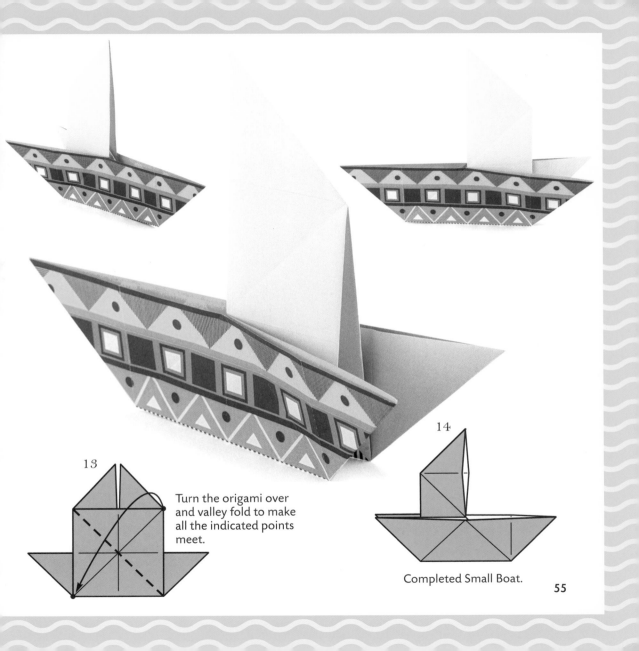

13

Turn the origami over and valley fold to make all the indicated points meet.

14

Completed Small Boat.

55

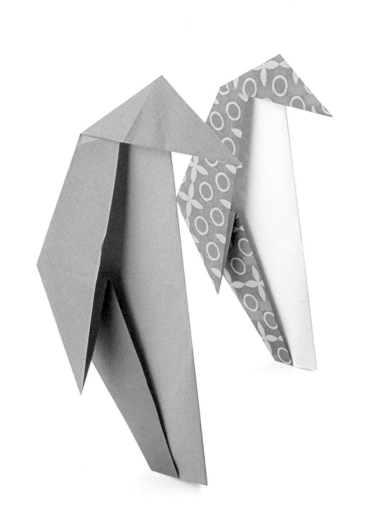

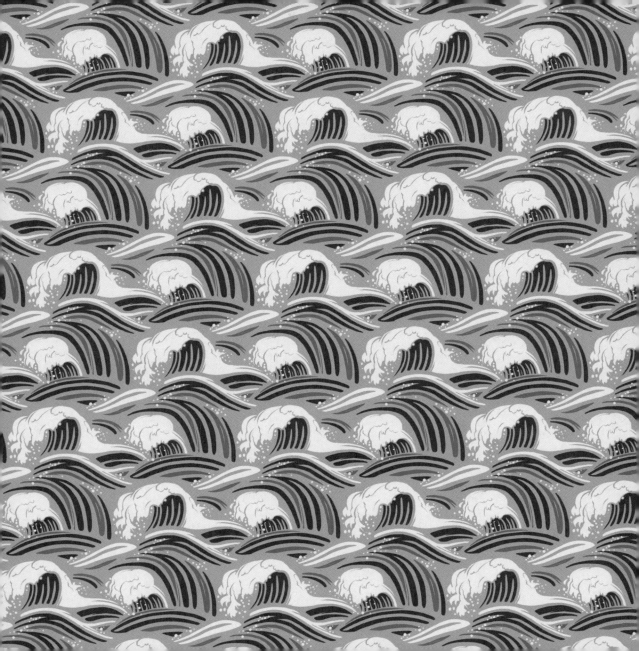

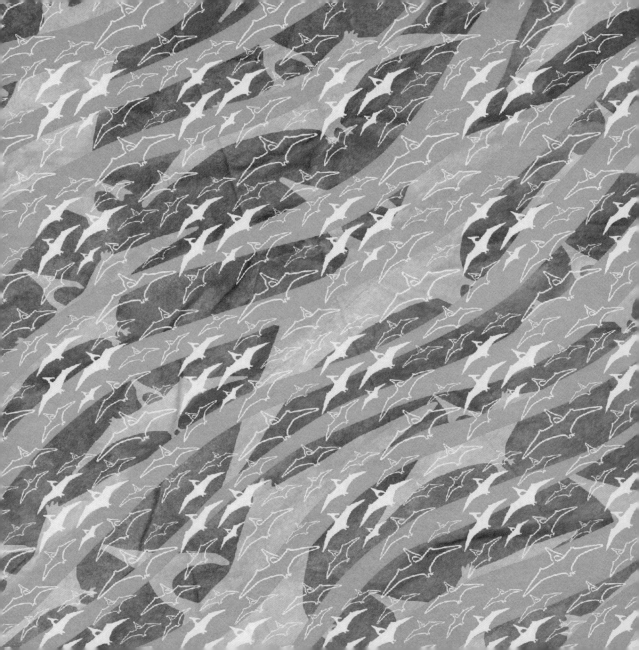

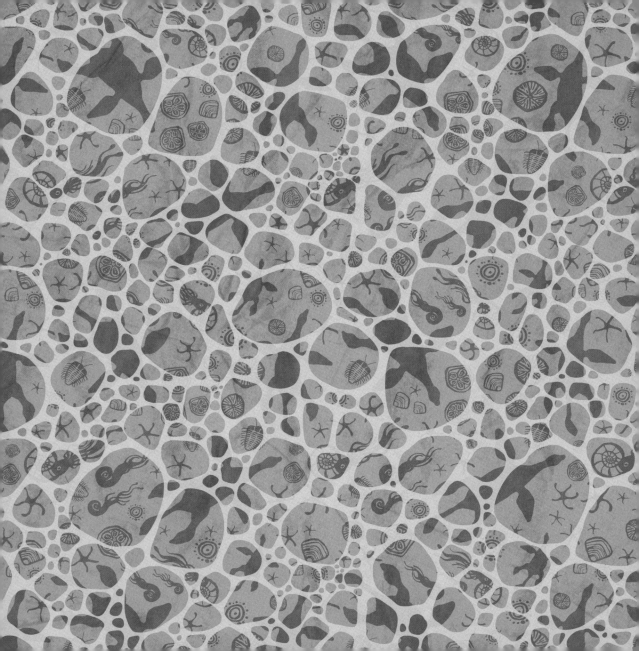

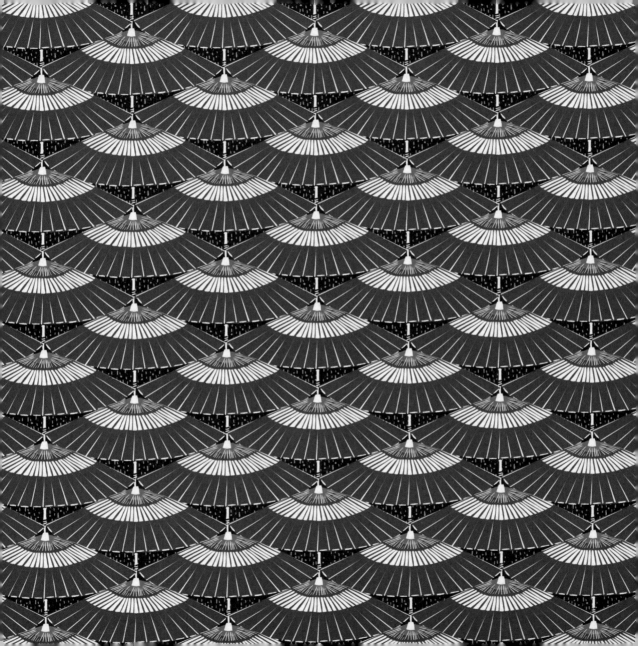

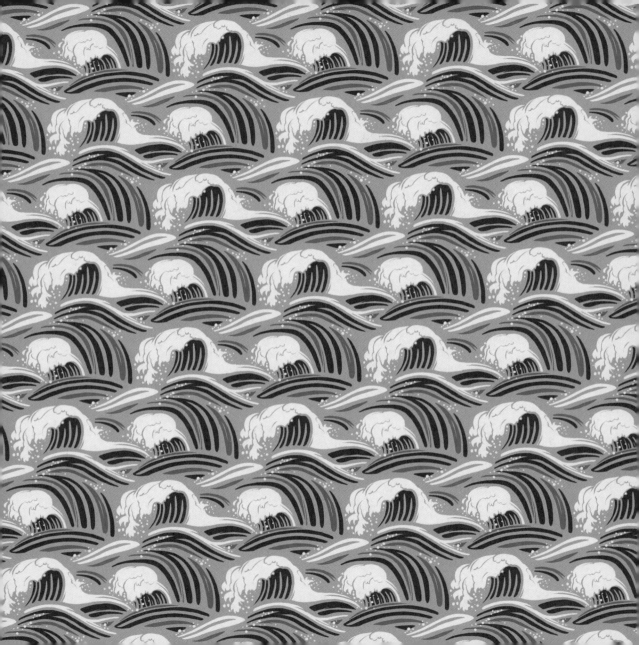

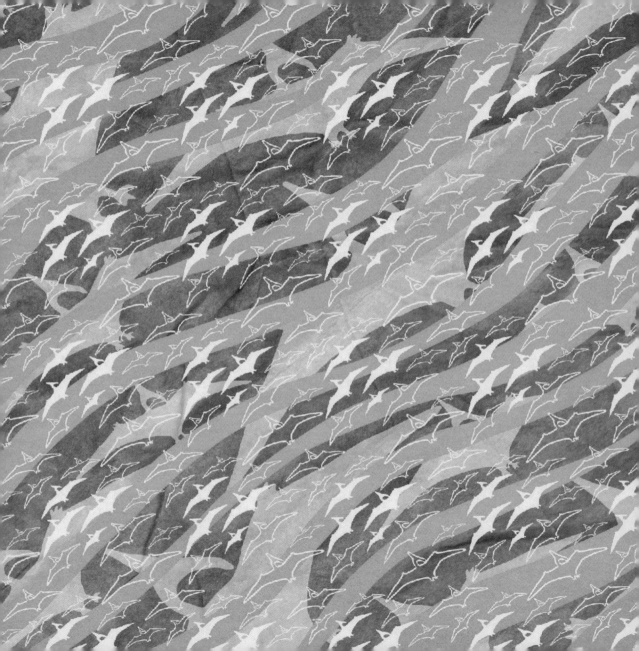

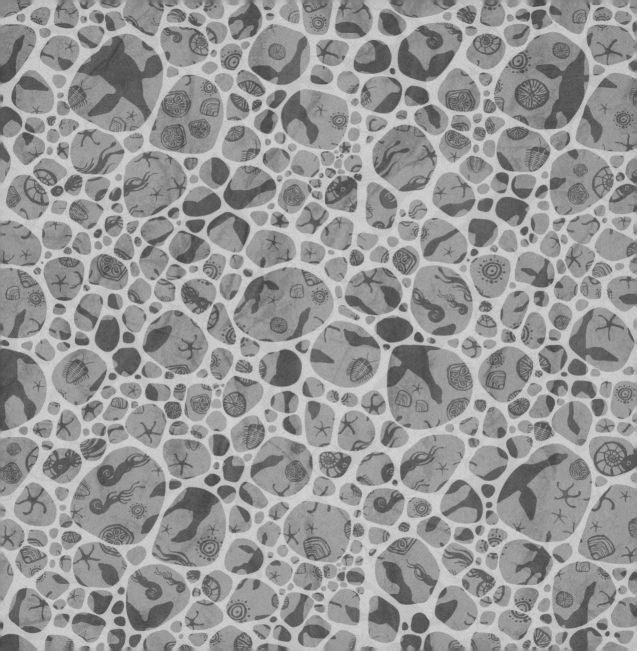

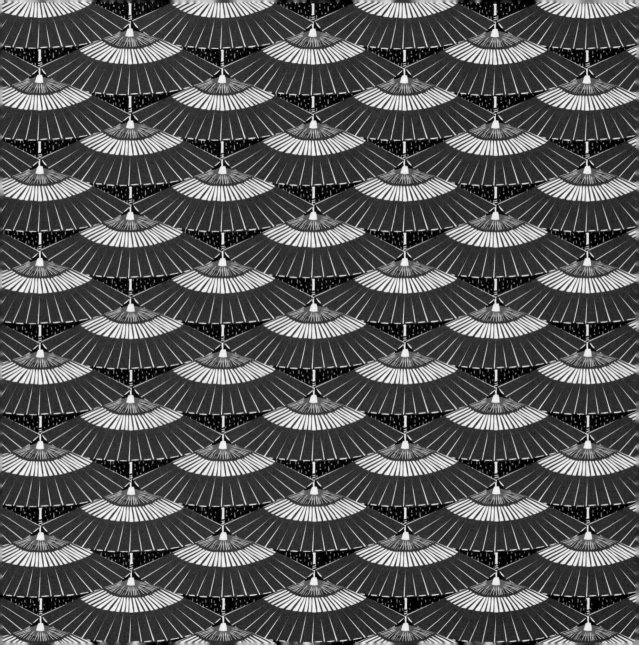

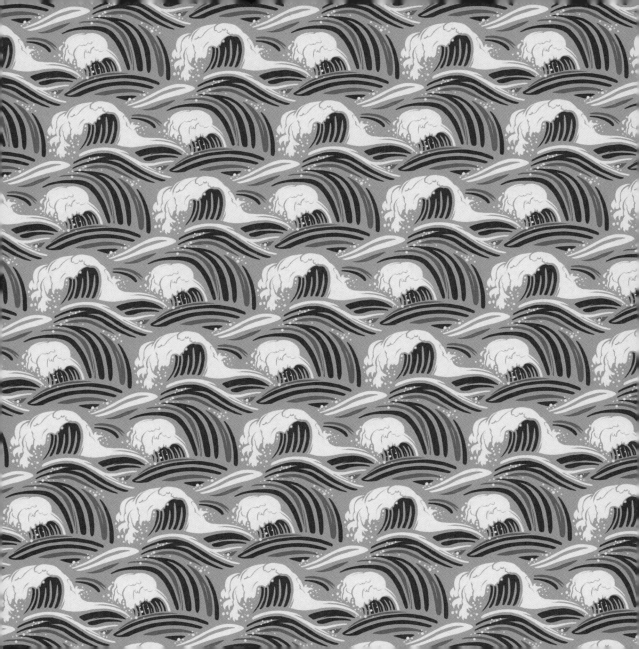

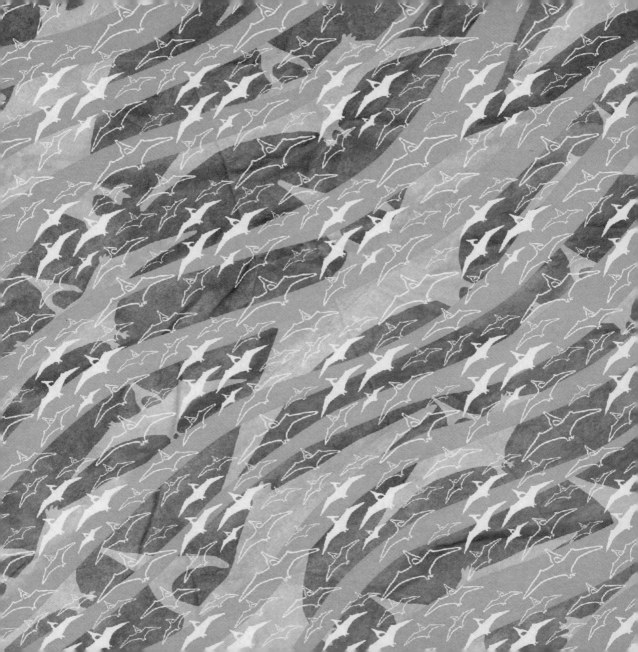

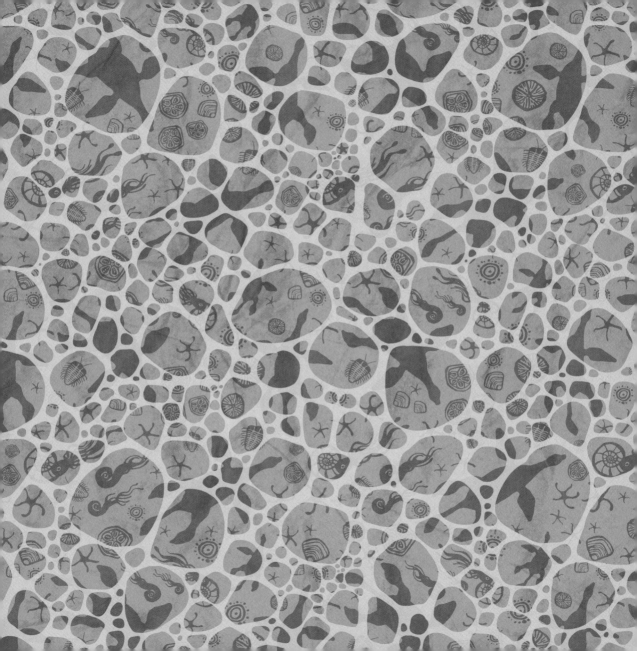

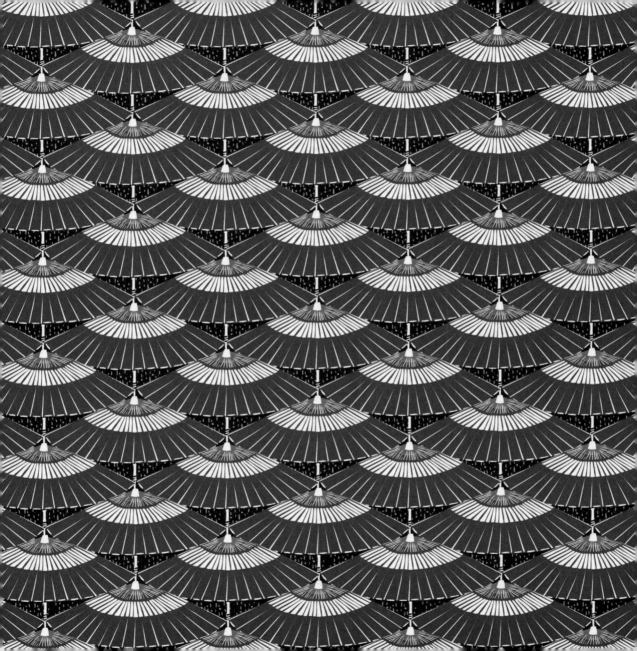

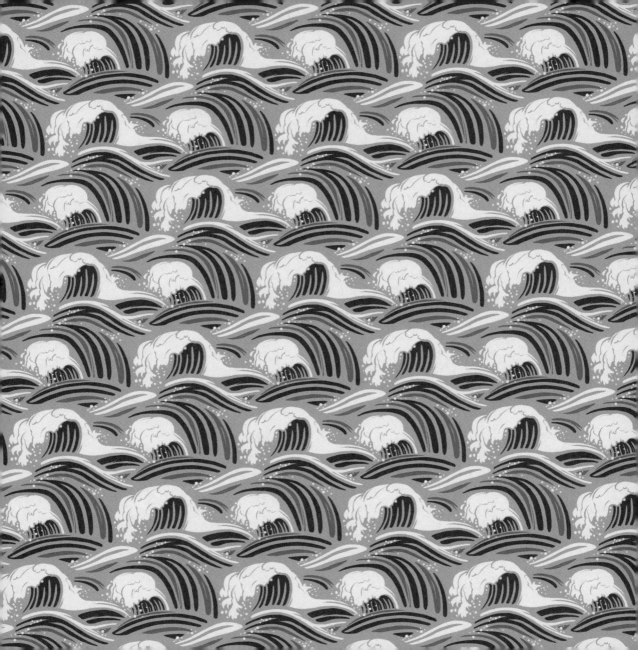

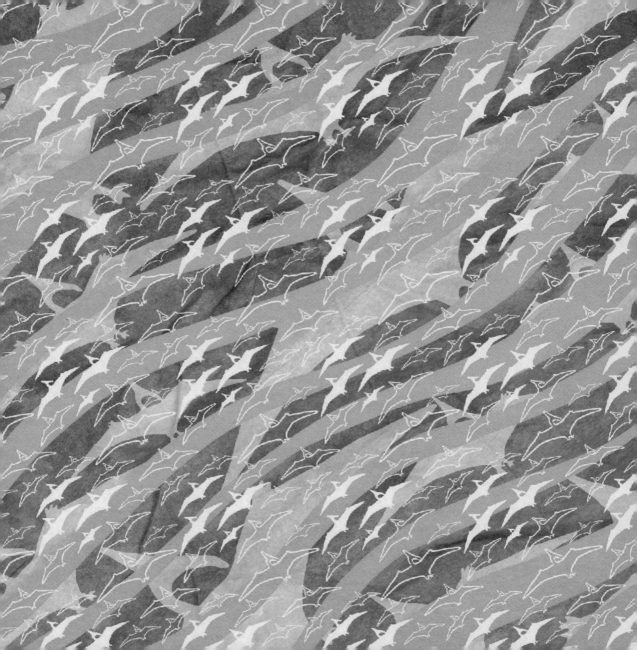

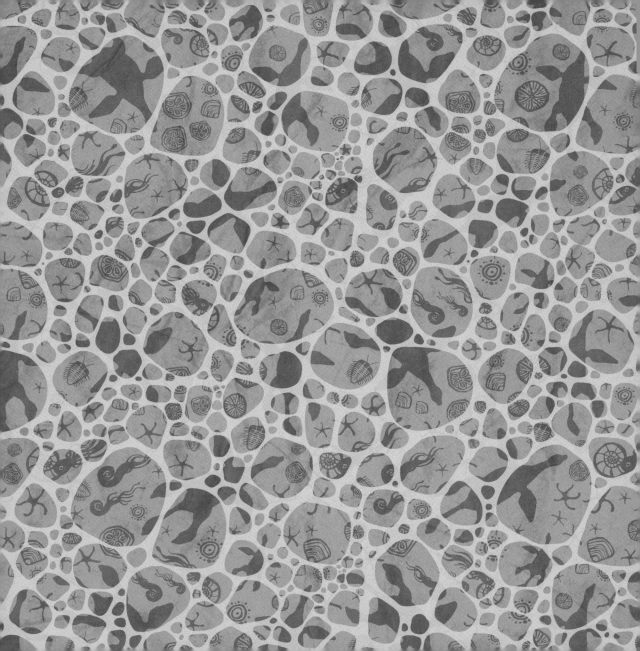

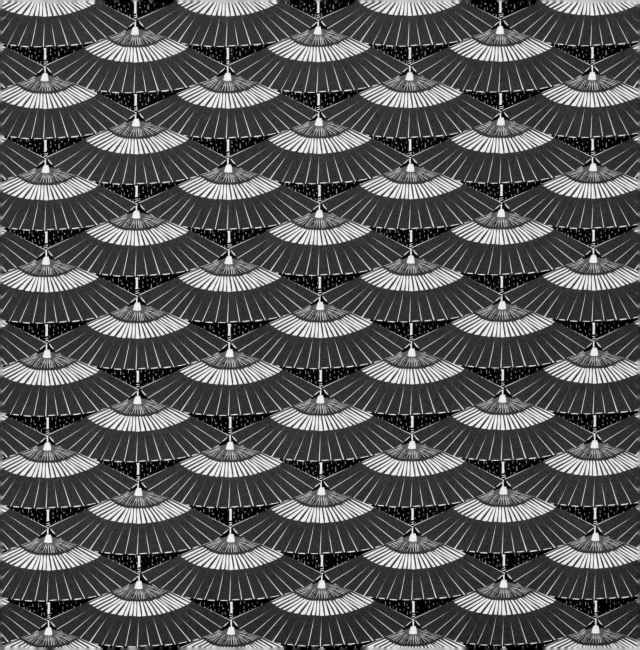

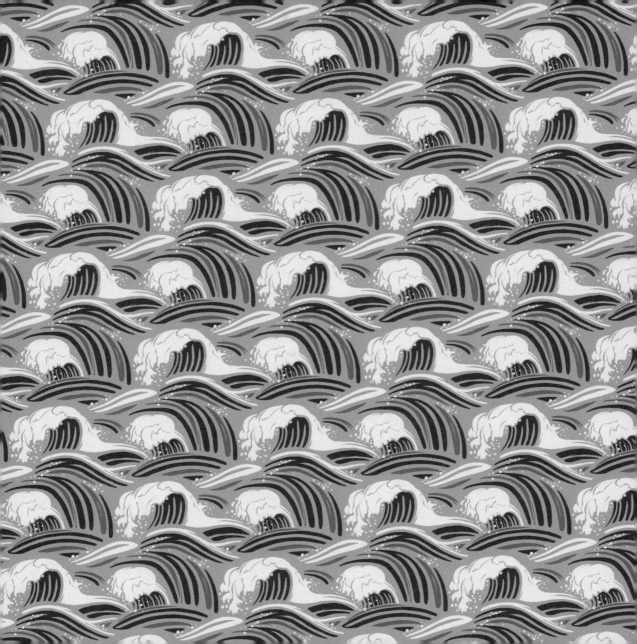

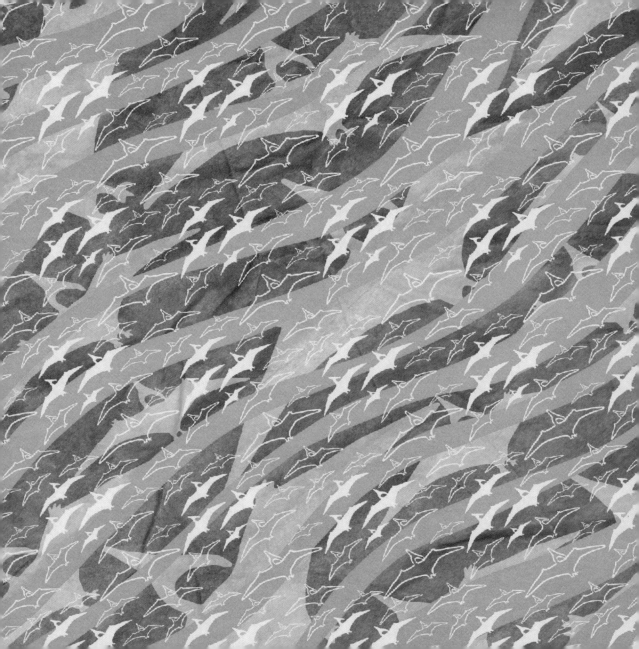

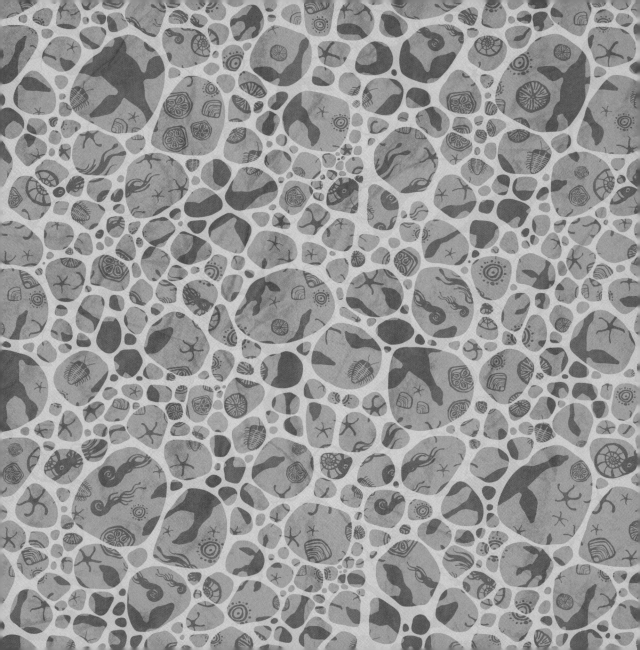